How to Play Funny Fill-In!

Love to create amazing stories? Good, because this one stars YOU. Get ready to laugh with all your friends—you can play with as many people as you want! Make sure to keep this book on your shelf. You'll want to read it again and again!

Are You Ready to Laugh?

- One person picks a story—you can start at the beginning, the middle, or the end of the book.

- Ask a friend to call out a word that the space asks for—noun, verb, or something else—and write it in the blank space. If there's more than one player, ask the next person to say a word. Extra points for creativity!

- When all the spaces are filled in, you have your very own Funny Fill-In. Read it out loud for a laugh.

- Want to play by yourself? Just fold over the page and use the cardboard insert at the back as a writing pad. Fill in the blank parts of speech list, and copy your answers into the story.

Fun Fact! Make sure you check out the amazing **Fun Facts** that appear on every page!

Parts of Speech

To play the game, you'll need to know how to form sentences. This list with examples of the parts of speech and other terms will help you get started:

Noun: The name of a person, place, thing, or idea
Examples: tree, mouth, creature
The **ocean** is full of colorful **fish**.

Adjective: A word that describes a noun or pronoun
Examples: green, lazy, friendly
My **silly** dog won't stop laughing!

Verb: An action word. In the present tense, a verb often ends in –s or –ing. If the space asks for past tense, changing the vowel or adding a –d or –ed to the end usually will set the sentence in the past.
Examples: swim, hide, plays, running (present tense); biked, rode, jumped (past tense)
The giraffe **skips** across the savanna.
The flower **opened** after the rain.

Adverb: A word that describes a verb and usually ends in –ly
Examples: quickly, lazily, soundlessly
Kelley **greedily** ate all the carrots.

Plural: More than one
Examples: mice, telephones, wrenches
Why are all the **doors** closing?

Silly Word or Exclamation: A funny sound, a made-up word, a word you think is totally weird, or a noise someone or something might make
Examples: Ouch! No way! Foozleduzzle! Yikes!
"Darn!" shouted Jim. "These cupcakes are sour!"

Specific Words: There are many more ways to make your story hilarious. When asked for something like a number, animal, or body part, write in something you think is especially funny.

- friend's name
  - noun
- celebrity name
  - adjective
- noun
  - adjective
- letter
  - number
- same friend
  - verb
- adverb ending in –ly
  - body part, plural
- exclamation
  - noun, plural
- adjective
  - ocean animal
- noun, plural
  - body part
- verb

Fun Fact! HYACINTH MACAWS, THE LARGEST TYPE OF PARROT, HAVE A WINGSPAN OF MORE THAN FOUR FEET (1.2 M).

Summer break has finally arrived! My friend _____ and I are building a sand

friend's name

_____ on _____ Beach. I dig into the _____ sand to fill my

noun   celebrity name   adjective

_____ and pull out a(n) _____ bottle. Inside is a treasure map with not one

noun   adjective

"_____ marks the spot," but _____ ! _____ and I _____

letter   number   same friend   verb

up and down when _____ a parrot swoops down and grabs the map from our

adverb ending in –ly

_____ . " _____ !" I cry as we chase the parrot down the beach, through

body part, plural   exclamation

trees and _____ . We round a corner and come across a ship called The _____

noun, plural   adjective

_____ . We can't believe our _____ . On the ship's bow is a pirate with the

ocean animal   noun, plural

parrot on his _____ . He waves and calls, "C'mon mateys, it's high time to _____ the seas!"

body part   verb

verb

large number

verb

adjective

verb ending in –ing

something gross

noun

verb

direction

body part

adjective

animal

your name

noun

adjective

your favorite color

your last name

noun, plural

number

Fun Fact! THE **YOUNGEST** KNOWN PIRATE WAS **NINE YEARS OLD.**

MAP

Pirate Makeover

We _____ aboard the ship and the captain says, "Let's get _____ things straight—
       verb   large number

you both need to learn to be pirates to _____ on this ship." He leads us to the main deck, where
                                              verb

_____ pirates are _____ by the cannons, all the way to the _____
      adjective   verb ending in –ing   something gross

deck, where the steering _____ is located. We _____ by the galley, infirmary, and
                              noun   verb

sleeping quarters then head _____ into the cargo hold. There we put on _____
                                 direction   body part

patches, bandanas, _____ boots, earrings, and temporary _____ skull tattoos.
                        adjective   animal

The captain then tells me that with a landlubber name like _____, I'll be walking the
                                                                your name

_____ in no time. _____ _____ _____ will be
      noun   adjective   your favorite color   your last name

my new name. With the ship's logbook in hand to keep track of _____, we are finally
                                                                    noun, plural

ready to explore the _____ seas for treasure!
                          number

noun

    direction

letter

    number

friend's name

    verb

noun

    type of house

noun, plural

    same letter

large number

    noun, plural

noun, plural

    adjective

same friend

    item of clothing

silly word

    favorite candy

verb

Fun Fact!

LOLLIPOP MACHINES
MAKE UP TO
5,900 LOLLIPOPS IN
ONE MINUTE.

I pull the treasure map out of my _____ and see we need to sail _____ to arrive at the
                                        noun   direction

first "_____." After _____ hours of sailing, we finally reach a deserted beach. _____
              letter   number   friend's name

and I _____ off the ship while the captain drops the _____ over the ship's side to
              verb   noun

make sure the ship stays put. The only thing in sight is a(n) _____ with _____
                                                                type of house   noun, plural

in the shape of a(n) _____ on the door—this must be the spot! It looks like no one has been here for
                        same letter

_____ _____ . Inside, the _____ on the windows are all closed, so
  large number   noun, plural   noun, plural

there is little light. The air feels very _____ . Suddenly, my foot breaks through the rotting
                                              adjective

floorboards! _____ grabs my _____ and pulls me out. "_____!"
                same friend   item of clothing   silly word

my friend yells. Under the floor is a room full of _____ and gold doubloons. We break
                                                        favorite candy

through and _____ all the way down the mound of treasure. What a sweet ride.
                verb

letter

   direction

adjective

   noun, plural

something sharp, plural

   something gross

item of clothing

   adjective

insect

   body part

verb

   vegetable, plural

color

   body part

animal

   adverb ending in –ly

musical instrument

   adjective

Fun Fact!

VENUS FLYTRAPS CAN TAKE AS MANY AS TEN DAYS TO DIGEST AN INSECT.

A Sparkle in the Swamp

Back on the ship we set sail for the next _____ on the treasure map. This time we anchor somewhere
letter

in the bogs of _____ Carolina. The area is _____ and slimy, with no hint of
direction   adjective

treasure in sight. We walk through leafy _____ and prickly _____.
noun, plural   something sharp, plural

_____ gets all over my boots, and mud squirts up onto my _____.
something gross   item of clothing

A(n) _____ _____ buzzes by my _____. Just as I am about to
adjective   insect   body part

_____ back to the ship, a gleam from a patch of _____ catches my eye.
verb   vegetable, plural

I run over and see a large _____ diamond stuck in the _____ of a(n) _____-eating
color   body part   animal

plant. _____, I play a(n) _____ to lull the carnivore to sleep, then I grab the
adverb ending in –ly   musical instrument

diamond and throw it into our treasure bag. We agree it is a much better find than a(n) _____ bug!
adjective

friend's name

　　color

type of furniture

　　noun, plural

silly noise

　　color

animal

　　large number

verb

　　adjective

noun

　　verb

shape

　　body part

number

　　same body part, plural

verb

　　liquid

Fun Fact! AN **OCTOPUS** CAN HAVE NEARLY **2,000 SUCKERS** ON ITS TENTACLES.

Tentacled Treasure

After finding some treasure, _____ and I decide to celebrate. We secure the map in Captain
                              friend's name

_____ Beard's _____ and head out to explore the sea. We grab diving gear and slide
   color   type of furniture

oxygen _____ over our heads. With a big _____ , we splash into the water. We look
         noun, plural   silly noise

down and see a sunken pirate ship! As we swim closer, we see a school of _____-finned _____
                                                                            color   animal

fish and a(n) _____-armed octopus following us. A little weirded out, we _____ through a broken
              large number   verb

window on the ship and see a(n) _____ chest wedged in the _____ . We tug on the treasure
                                   adjective   noun

chest with all our strength, but it doesn't _____ . Then a(n) _____ octopus _____
                                              verb   shape   body part

slides by me and grabs our booty! _____ more _____ attach to the chest, and we
                                    number   same body part, plural

watch the octopus wiggle and _____ until the chest comes free and crashes open on the
                              verb

seafloor. That scares the octopus—it immediately squirts _____ and swims away.
                                                            liquid

13

noun

adverb

adjective

silly noise

color

verb

friend's name

kitchen utensil

verb

liquid

adverb

adjective

adjective

favorite animal

adjective

exclamation

color

adjective

Fun Fact!

A MAN FROM SANTA FE, NEW MEXICO, U.S.A., HID A BOX OF TREASURE WORTH $1 MILLION IN THE ROCKY MOUNTAINS THAT HAS YET TO BE FOUND.

14

Liquid Gold

With the treasure chest on the ship's _____ (noun), I struggle _____ (adverb) to open the lid.

The pirate _____ (adjective) Bones Johnson lends a hook hand. Finally, the chest swings open with a

_____ (silly noise). Inside, it's filled with _____ (color) and gold coins! I don't _____ (verb) for long because

the coins I pick up melt in my hand. _____ (friend's name) scoops up a handful using a(n) _____ (kitchen utensil).

They also melt. Every coin we _____ (verb) melts immediately. Soon, all that's left is a puddle of gold

_____ (liquid). _____ (adverb), I reach into the chest of _____ (adjective) goo and feel something

solid. I bring it out to find it's a(n) _____ (adjective) key in the shape of a(n) _____ (favorite animal).

I remember seeing a similar key on the _____ (adjective) map and unroll it to check. "_____ (exclamation)!" I cry.

A picture of the same key is now glowing _____ (color), along with three other key outlines. Our adventure

just got much more _____ (adjective).

- silly word
  - verb
- adjective
  - adjective
- noun
  - something creepy, plural
- noun, plural
  - favorite number
- adverb ending in –ly
  - noun
- adjective
  - letter
- adjective
  - adverb ending in –ly
- silly word
  - verb
- favorite toy
  - favorite candy bar
- favorite band

Fun Fact! GEOCACHING IS A TREASURE HUNTING GAME IN WHICH PLAYERS USE A GPS TO LOCATE ITEMS HIDDEN BY OTHER PLAYERS.

The next stop on the map is an island in the Bahamas called _____ . Once we _____
_____silly word_____ _____verb_____

on the island, all we see is a dark, _____ cave. I take a(n) _____ breath, grab a
_____adjective_____ _____adjective_____

_____ , and walk in. _____ and spider _____ line the cave
_____noun_____ ____something creepy, plural____ _____noun, plural_____

walls. After _____ hours, we come to a dead end. "Did we miss the treasure?" I ask and lean
_____favorite number_____

_____ against the wall. It moves! I shine a(n) _____ on the wall and see
____adverb ending in –ly____ _____noun_____

_____ bricks arranged in the shape of a(n) _____ . We push all of the _____
_____adjective_____ _____letter_____ _____adjective_____

bricks in, and the entire wall _____ opens. "_____ !" I yell as coins and gems
____adverb ending in –ly____ _____silly word_____

_____ out, along with a(n) _____ , _____ , and tickets to
_____verb_____ _____favorite toy_____ _____favorite candy bar_____

see _____ . We definitely hit the jackpot!
_____favorite band_____

- verb
  - vegetable, plural
- adjective
  - color
- color
  - celebrity name
- animal, plural
  - noun, plural
- number
  - yard tool
- friend's name
  - gemstone
- verb
  - kitchen appliance
- verb ending in –ing
  - dance move
- silly word
  - adjective
- noun

PIRATES MUST HAVE **LOVED MUSIC!** ANY MUSICIANS **THEY CAPTURED** WERE FORCED TO **JOIN THE CREW.**

Fun Fact!

Island Jam

We _____(verb)_____ all the way to Jamaica while eating tropical _____(vegetable, plural)_____ and _____(adjective)_____ fruit. Captain _____(color)_____ Beard and his crew start to cheer when we hear music coming from a(n) _____(color)_____ shack on the beach. Playing this evening is the famous band _____(celebrity name)_____ and The Island _____(animal, plural)_____. The band has drums made from _____(noun, plural)_____, guitars, and a(n) _____(number)_____-stringed _____(yard tool)_____. _____(friend's name)_____ spots what looks like a giant _____(gemstone)_____ on the floor behind the band. We move closer to see, but before I can _____(verb)_____ it we are pulled into the band and given _____(kitchen appliance)_____ instruments to play. I jump around the stage _____(verb ending in –ing)_____ my instrument and doing the _____(dance move)_____ while my friend sings "_____(silly word)_____" off-key. We have so much fun we forget about the gemstone until the evening turns _____(adjective)_____. It turns out the "gem" was just a shiny _____(noun)_____ anyway.

- verb
  - direction
- animal
  - same animal
- color
  - number
- object in space
  - exclamation
- noun, plural
  - favorite color
- noun, plural
  - adjective
- something soft
  - silly noise
- gemstone
  - superhero
- adverb ending in −ly
  - adjective

Fun Fact! THERE ARE MORE STARS IN THE UNIVERSE THAN GRAINS OF SAND ON EARTH.

As night falls, we _____ back to the ship. The map says to head _____ between the North
   verb   direction

Star and the _____ constellation. We scan the sky and spot a cluster of stars that looks just like
                animal

a(n) _____ . Captain _____ Beard sets course in that direction, going _____
      same animal   color   number

nautical miles an hour. Soon we are using the light of the _____ to steer by. "_____ !"
                                                            object in space   exclamation

the captain says breathlessly. Before us is an island of luxury and _____ . We are surrounded
                                                                     noun, plural

by _____ sparkles and fluffy _____ , and there's a(n) _____ swimming pool.
    favorite color   noun, plural   adjective

I run to a giant bed with _____ sheets and plop down with a(n) _____ . Yawning,
                           something soft   silly noise

I lie back on a pillow. Ouch! Underneath the pillow is a(n) _____-encrusted key in the shape
                                                             gemstone

of _____ . One of the keys we have been looking for! I flop _____ back
    superhero   adverb ending in –ly

down on the comfy bed. We will have a(n) _____ day tomorrow.
                                          adjective

- adjective
- verb
- noun
- color
- adjective
- noun
- noun, plural
- noun, plural
- animal, plural
- bird, plural
- noun, plural
- silly noise
- friend's name
- body part, plural
- adjective
- ocean animal, plural

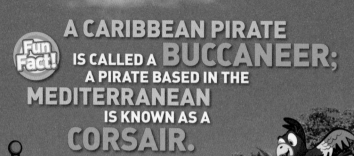

Fun Fact! A CARIBBEAN PIRATE IS CALLED A **BUCCANEER;** A PIRATE BASED IN THE **MEDITERRANEAN** IS KNOWN AS A **CORSAIR.**

All Paws on Deck

Early in the morning, everyone wakes up to the _____ light of the sun. I _____ around
                                              (adjective)   (verb)

the cozy Caribbean island—and see the ship in the distance! It must have drifted away overnight. We'll need

to build a(n) _____ to get back to the ship. Using _____ leaves and _____ roots,
              (noun)   (color)   (adjective)

the crew gets to work. We discover that wood from the _____ tree floats well. We make a sail from
                                                      (noun)

_____ . We fill the finished raft with coconuts and _____ for the trip. Some of
(noun, plural)   (noun, plural)

the island's residents help us launch it. _____ help slide the raft into the ocean. Toucans
                                          (animal, plural)

and _____ grab the sail with their beaks and flap their _____ , making
    (bird, plural)   (noun, plural)

the loudest _____ . _____ and I hop on with the others. Holding
            (silly noise)   (friend's name)

_____ , we hope for _____ sailing. _____ and stingrays push
(body part, plural)   (adjective)   (ocean animal, plural)

the raft from behind. Before too long, we're safely on board the ship again!

letter

adjective

adjective

yard tool, plural

body part

silly word

animal

adjective

number

noun

adjective

animal

liquid

same letter

verb

same liquid

noun

noun, plural

adjective

Fun Fact!

THE WORLD'S TALLEST WATERFALL, ANGEL FALLS IN VENEZUELA, IS TALLER THAN FIVE WASHINGTON MONUMENTS.

Off to the next _____ on the map! We sail farther south, toward the _____ rain forests
                    letter   adjective

of Brazil. These rain forests are dense and _____ . We'll need our swords and _____
                                              adjective   yard tool, plural

to create a trail. A tarantula runs across my _____ as I step off the ship. "_____ !" I cry.
                                                body part   silly word

We pass by a poison dart _____ and a(n) _____ snake. Above us a(n) _____ -toed
                          animal   adjective   number

sloth hangs from a(n) _____ . We reach a river and cross a(n) _____ -looking bridge
                        noun   adjective

high up in the air. Somewhere in the distance a spotted _____ roars. Finally, we arrive at some
                                                          animal

_____ falls. I tell my friend, "Look, this is where _____ marks the spot." I _____
  liquid   same letter   verb

into the _____ falls and feel only empty space behind it. I cover my _____ and
          same liquid   noun

race through it. The ground behind the falls is covered in gold _____
                                                                 noun, plural

and _____ jewelry. Good thing we brought bags!
     adjective

25

SMALLEST MONKEY—
THE PYGMY MARMOSET—
AND THE LOUDEST—
THE HOWLER MONKEY.

body part, plural

verb

exclamation

adjective

large number

favorite song

adverb

verb

noun, plural

favorite candy

type of clothing, plural

verb ending in –s

verb ending in –s

color

silly word

noun, plural

noun, plural

verb

Monkey Madness

With our _____ (body part, plural) full of treasure, we _____ (verb) back to the ship. "_____ (exclamation)!"

my friend yells. "There are _____ (adjective) monkeys aboard!" Sure enough, the ship has been taken over

by _____ (large number) monkeys. They are singing the pirate shanty "_____ (favorite song)" and dancing

_____ (adverb) on the deck. There's treasure everywhere. I watch as they _____ (verb) around

in it and throw pearl _____ (noun, plural) and gold _____ (favorite candy) into the air. They have found

the stored pirate gear, and most are wearing pirate _____ (type of clothing, plural) on their heads. A troop of monkeys

_____ (verb ending in –s) up the ship's mast. One gets stuck in the rope netting and _____ (verb ending in –s)

upside down. "Make some noise!" shouts Captain _____ (color) Beard. I run onto the ship yelling,

"_____ (silly word)!" while my friend bangs _____ (noun, plural) and _____ (noun, plural) together.

All the monkeys _____ (verb) off the ship. Talk about monkeying around!

color

　adjective

noun

　adjective

animal, plural

　animal, plural

liquid

　noun

noun, plural

　noun, plural

verb

　exclamation

verb ending in –s

　celebrity name

adjective

　adverb ending in –ly

noun, plural

　body part

number

Fun Fact! THERE ARE ABOUT **2,000 THUNDERSTORMS** HAPPENING SOMEWHERE ON EARTH **AT ANY TIME.**

Storm at Sea

The sky suddenly turns dark _____ and cloudy. Large, _____ waves begin to rock
color _adjective_

the ship. A bright flash of _____ streaks across the sky. Before we know it, we're caught in
noun

a(n) _____ storm! It starts raining _____ and _____ . Large drops of
adjective _animal, plural_ _animal, plural_

_____ hit the deck and soak through my _____ . Barrels filled with _____
liquid _noun_ _noun, plural_

roll around the deck. A wave filled with crabs and _____ crashes over the railing.
noun, plural

I slip on seaweed and _____ into the ship's steering wheel. "_____ !" I yell as the ship
verb _exclamation_

_____ in the wrong direction. A pirate who looks just like _____ picks me up.
verb ending in –s _celebrity name_

It's too _____ to stay on deck. Everyone runs _____ for shelter, dodging loose
adjective _adverb ending in –ly_

cannonballs and _____ , but we make it. There is a crab clinging to my friend's _____ .
noun, plural _body part_

After _____ days the storm ends. We can explore once more.
number

- verb ending in –s
  - silly word
- adjective
  - friend's name
- verb
  - noun
- noun, plural
  - something sparkly
- adjective
  - type of nut, plural
- type of flower, plural
  - color
- fruit
  - noun
- animal, plural
  - adjective
- adjective
  - precious gem
- body part, plural

Fun Fact! TREASURE ISLAND IS A SMALL MAN-MADE ISLAND OFF CALIFORNIA, U.S.A.

Treasure Island

Now off course, the ship _____ into a strange island. "_____," I say. The captain
                             verb ending in −s   *silly word*

and his crew member _____ Bones Jones need to adjust the ship's helm, so _____
                            adjective   *friend's name*

and I _____ off the ship to explore. The island appears to be made of treasure and _____.
          verb   *noun*

The _____ have leaves made of emerald and _____. Their bark is
       noun, plural   *something sparkly*

_____ bronze, and their seeds are huge gold doubloons instead of _____.
    adjective   *type of nut, plural*

What look like _____ turn out to be _____ pearl strands. There is a golden
                type of flower, plural   *color*

_____ tree and a silver _____ bush. Diamond-spotted _____ cross our path.
    fruit   *noun*   *animal, plural*

Ruby-eyed toucans drink water from a(n) _____ pond. A bronze tortoise walks by with a(n)
                                            adjective

_____ shell. Overhead are parrots with _____ beaks and gold _____.
    adjective   *precious gem*   *body part, plural*

On an island of treasure, there is none to be taken.

- adjective
  - animal
- noun
  - body part, plural
- adjective
  - liquid
- adjective
  - color
- noun, plural
  - silly word
- adjective
  - verb ending in –s
- adverb ending in –ly
  - verb
- body part
  - adjective
- letter
  - yard tool, plural
- favorite flavor

Fun Fact! THE **HIGHEST DUNES** IN THE **SAHARA** ARE TALLER THAN THE **EMPIRE STATE BUILDING** IN NEW YORK CITY, U.S.A.

Using our _____ compass, we steer the ship toward the _____ Desert of Africa.
adjective   animal

We slather on sunscreen from a(n) _____ so our _____ won't burn. The ship
noun   body part, plural

makes anchor, but we see nothing but _____ dunes for miles. The entire crew decides to head
adjective

out. We bring _____ bottles to stay hydrated. The sun is hot and _____ above.
liquid   adjective

Ahead is a patch of _____ cactus and desert _____ . "_____!" _____
color   noun, plural   silly word   adjective

Legs Pete cries as the wind picks up and sand _____ around. My hat _____
verb ending in –s   adverb ending in –ly

flies away. I _____ after it through a herd of hump-_____ camels. The hat finally
verb   body part

lands on the _____ ground. I pick it up, and underneath it is a(n) _____ from the
adjective   letter

treasure map! We dig in the sand using _____ . To our delight, we find a cooler full of
yard tool, plural

_____ ice cream. Yum, desert dessert!
favorite flavor

- relative's name
  - noun
- something scary
  - color
- friend's name
  - number
- verb
  - adjective
- favorite color
  - noun
- silly word
  - another color
- adjective
  - adjective
- verb
  - adverb ending in –ly
- adjective

Fun Fact! BLACK AND WHITE ARE NOT TRUE COLORS.

Next up, we sail north through the Strait of _____ and into the Mediterranean _____ .
        relative's name   noun

We land on the coast of a European country that looks like a(n) _____ . Captain _____
                                                        something scary   color

Beard and crew leave my friend _____ and me with the map. After _____ hours
                    friend's name   number

walking alone, we _____ across a shack painted black and white. We open the _____
                verb   adjective

door and peek inside. I step into the room, and suddenly the floor turns bright _____ !
                                                                            favorite color

My friend picks up a(n) _____ from the table, and it turns purple. I lean into the table and
                    noun

" _____ !" it turns _____ ! Everything we touch turns a(n) _____ color—
    silly word   another color   adjective

except for a spatula that remains gray. On the _____ floor we see a gray patch. I _____
                                            adjective   verb

at my friend and know what we have to do. We dig _____ , using the spatula, and reveal
                                            adverb ending in –ly

another key! This one is rainbow colored and _____ .
                                        adjective

- friend's name
  - room
- gross food
  - number
- verb
  - favorite food, plural
- liquid
  - type of food
- your age
  - noun
- adjective
  - noun
- vegetable, plural
  - spice
- noun
  - verb ending in –ing
- favorite singer
  - food

Fun Fact! CATS WERE KEPT ABOARD SHIPS TO HELP KEEP RODENTS AWAY FROM FOOD SUPPLIES.

Pirate Appetite

_____ and I are getting hungry back aboard the ship. We look around the _____
    friend's name   room

for food. There is only dry bread and _____ . Since we have eaten that for dinner the last
                                             gross food

_____ nights, we _____ to the galley in hopes of finding _____ .
   number   verb   favorite food, plural

We walk inside and hear some pirates singing, "Yo ho ho and a bottle of _____ !" Coconut juice
                                                             liquid

and _____ are flying everywhere. A(n) _____-year-old pirate is banging on a(n)
             type of food   your age

_____ and pots with a sword. We can't resist joining the fun. A pot of _____ stew is
   noun   adjective

cooking on the _____ . We throw _____, _____ , and pieces
                 noun   vegetable, plural   spice

of _____ in with a splash. The crew starts _____ _____'s
   noun   verb ending in –ing   favorite singer

latest song. We sing shanties and eat _____ all night.
                                         food

color

　　adjective

verb

　　friend's name

adjective

　　something huge

adjective

　　noun, plural

verb ending in –s

　　large number

verb

　　animal, plural

adjective

　　adjective

noun, plural

　　noun

verb ending in –s

　　adjective

MADAGASCAR IS HOME TO SOME 100 SPECIES OF LEMURS.

Jungle Gem

In the morning, Captain _____ Beard cruises through the _____ Canal and sails for
          color   adjective

Madagascar. Once we land, it's off to _____ for treasure. The captain's parrot squawks, "Good
                                              verb

luck!" to _____ and me. We walk past _____ trees and a chameleon as big as a(n)
          friend's name   adjective

_____ . Deep in the _____ jungle, we uncover a large, hidden sapphire.
   something huge   adjective

"Shiver me _____ !" I yell as a lemur _____ the gem. He's not alone—there are
              noun, plural   verb ending in –s

_____ lemurs surrounding us. We _____ into the trees like _____
   large number   verb   animal, plural

after them. I think I spot a(n) _____ lemur tail and grab it. It turns out to be a(n) _____
                                   adjective   adjective

snake instead! We swing on _____ through the trees, chasing the lemur troop. Finally,
                              noun, plural

we corner them in a(n) _____ . The one with the sapphire _____ and laughs as
                            noun   verb ending in –s

he tosses the gem back. It was all just a(n) _____ game to them.
                                                adjective

- adjective
  - adjective
- noun, plural
  - adjective
- food
  - verb
- body part
  - adjective
- color
  - friend's name
- type of furniture
  - card game
- adjective
  - large number
- adjective
  - verb ending in –ing
- verb
  - noun, plural

Fun Fact! IN A DECK OF PLAYING CARDS, ONLY **THREE** OF THE **FOUR KINGS** HAVE **MUSTACHES.**

Below deck, the crew is throwing a(n) _____ party to celebrate their pirate holiday, _____
                                          adjective   adjective

Barnacle Day. The room is decorated with seaweed and _____ . Salty _____
                                                          noun, plural   adjective

punch is being served, along with crackers and crab _____ . I _____ as a pirate gets
                                                          food   verb

his wooden _____ stuck in the dance floor. The captain is throwing darts with _____
                body part   adjective

Pirate Pete and Sally _____ Beard. _____ and I sit down at a(n) _____
                          color   friend's name   type of furniture

to play _____ . I am dealt a(n) _____ hand with _____ aces
            card game   adjective   large number

and two kings. I bet half of my _____ coins. Then a pirate bets me with the last treasure
                                    adjective

key we've been _____ for! I have to _____ to win and bet all I have left.
                  verb ending in –ing   verb

My hand beats the other pirate's _____ of spades.
                                    noun, plural

We've found all four keys!

adjective

    friend's name

adverb ending in –ly

    noun

exclamation

    verb

noun

    verb ending in –ing

number

    adjective

adjective

    celebrity

adverb

    adjective ending in –est

verb ending in –s

    adjective

adjective

    noun

Fun Fact! ONLY **ONE** OUT OF EVERY **10,000 WILD MOLLUSKS** CONTAINS A **PEARL.**

Overboard!

Somewhere in the _____ Ocean near Australia, _____ and I celebrate the
adjective   friend's name

treasure we've found. We dance _____ until we trip over a(n) _____ on deck.
adverb ending in –ly   noun

"_____!" I cry as we both _____ overboard. Good thing we had our dive gear on! We see a
exclamation   verb

pod of _____-nose dolphins glide by below us. They swim over and instead of _____
noun   verb ending in –ing

us to the ship, they push us deeper underwater. _____ feet below we see the Great _____
number   adjective

Reef. There in the coral is a huge, _____ clamshell with a mermaid sitting nearby. She looks
adjective

just like _____! I swim over, and the clamshell opens _____. Inside is the
celebrity   adverb

_____ pearl I've ever seen. The mermaid hands the pearl to me and _____
adjective ending in –est   verb ending in –s

away. Then the _____ dolphins take us back to the ship. They use their _____
adjective   adjective

snouts to fling us up in the _____ and onto the deck. I'll take a dolphin over a diving board any day!
noun

43

- adjective
  - noun, plural
- adjective
  - utensil, plural
- yard tool, plural
  - silly word
- type of pattern
  - something huge
- adjective
  - favorite color
- shape
  - adverb ending in –ly
- same utensil
  - large number
- color
  - adjective
- verb

44

Wild Whale

It's a(n) _____ day, perfect for exploring. We decide to take the lifeboat out and explore the
      adjective

_____ of Australia. The ocean is smooth and _____ . We row the boat with
   noun, plural   adjective

_____ and _____ . " _____ !" I cry. From out of nowhere
   utensil, plural   yard tool, plural   silly word

a huge _____ whale appears. He is larger than a(n) _____ . _____
        type of pattern   something huge   adjective

air shoots out of his blowhole. With bright _____ _____ eyes, he looks at us
                                              favorite color   shape

_____ . He rocks the boat, and I drop my _____ paddle. We start spinning
  adverb ending in –ly   same utensil

at _____ miles an hour until I turn a shade of _____ . Suddenly, the boat stops moving.
   large number   color

Our _____ ocean friend disappears from view. He returns with my paddle and waves goodbye
      adjective

with a splash of his tail. Confused but excited, we watch him _____ away.
                                                              verb

letter

   adjective

animal

   verb

large number

   adjective

adverb ending in –ly

   favorite animal

adjective

   noun

verb ending in –s

   adjective

adverb

   noun

adjective

   adjective

silly word

   your hometown

Fun Fact!

ONE 400-YEAR-OLD
PIRATE TREASURE CHEST
WEIGHS 150 POUNDS (68 KG) —
WITHOUT ANY LOOT IN IT.

Another Adventure Awaits

We're off to search for the last and largest _____ (letter) on the _____ (adjective) map. We arrive at _____ (animal) Island and _____ (verb) off the ship, ready to explore. _____ (large number) hours later, we arrive at a cave with a(n) _____ (adjective) door filled with keyholes. _____ (adverb ending in –ly), I pull out all four keys from our worldwide treasure hunt. One keyhole in the door is shaped just like a(n) _____ (favorite animal), and a key fits perfectly. Another keyhole matches a different _____ (adjective) key. The third fits in the _____ (noun)-shaped hole. The door _____ (verb ending in –s) open. We peer in and see a(n) _____ (adjective) tunnel. I crawl _____ (adverb) down to find an empty room—except for an old chest sitting on a wooden _____ (noun). The last _____ (adjective) superhero key fits! The chest opens. Lying inside is another _____ (adjective) treasure map! "_____ (silly word)!" I exclaim. I think I'll say goodbye to the crew and head home to _____ (your hometown) and rest before setting sail again.

Credits

Cover: (water), mexrix/shutterstock; (ship), Avaglass/Dreamstime; (treasure chest), Litetender/ Dreamstime; 4, simonbradfield/iStockphoto; 6, HAYKIRDI/iStockphoto; 8, topora/Shutterstock; 10, John Oakey/Alamy; 12, Predrag Vuckovic/Getty Images; 14, Alex Tihonov/Dreamstime; 16, salajean/ iStockphoto; 18, Pikoso.kz/Shutterstock; 20, piskunov/iStockphoto; 22, Tommy Schultz/Dreamstime; 24, The Whiteview/Shutterstock; 26, Sebastian Czapnik/Dreamstime; 28, Alexander Lvov/Dreamstime; 30, Maria Skaldina/Shutterstock; 32, BremecR/iStockphoto; 34, Rodney Keaney/Shutterstock; 36, Kumar Sriskandan/Alamy; 38, Anrodphoto/iStockphoto; 40, Jean-Pierre Lescourret/Getty Images; 42, paul cowell/Shutterstock; 44, fabio fersa/Shutterstock; 46, Sinisa Botas/Shutterstock

Published by the National Geographic Society

John M. Fahey, *Chairman of the Board and Chief Executive Officer*

Declan Moore, *Executive Vice President; President, Publishing and Travel*

Melina Gerosa Bellows, *Publisher and Chief Creative Officer, Books, Kids, and Family*

Prepared by the Book Division

Hector Sierra, *Senior Vice President and General Manager*

Nancy Laties Feresten, *Senior Vice President, Kids Publishing and Media*

Jennifer Emmett, *Vice President, Editorial Director, Kids Books*

Eva Absher-Schantz, *Design Director, Kids Publishing and Media*

Jay Sumner, *Director of Photography, Kids Publishing*

R. Gary Colbert, *Production Director*

Jennifer A. Thornton, *Director of Managing Editorial*

Staff for This Book

Kate Olesin, *Project Editor*

James Hiscott Jr., *Art Director*

Kelley Miller, *Senior Photo Editor*

Ruth Ann Thompson, *Designer*

Bianca Bowman, *Writer*

Jason Tharp, *Illustrator*

Bri Bertoia, *Freelance Photo Editor*

Ariane Szu-Tu, *Editorial Assistant*

Callie Broaddus, *Design Production Assistant*

Margaret Leist, *Photo Assistant*

Grace Hill, *Associate Managing Editor*

Joan Gossett, *Production Editor*

Lewis R. Bassford, *Production Manager*

Susan Borke, *Legal and Business Affairs*

Production Services

Phillip L. Schlosser, *Senior Vice President*

Chris Brown, *Vice President, NG Book Manufacturing*

George Bounelis, *Senior Production Manager*

Nicole Elliott, *Director of Production*

Rachel Faulise, *Manager*

Robert L. Barr, *Manager*

The National Geographic Society is one of the world's largest nonprofit scientific and educational organizations. Founded in 1888 to "increase and diffuse geographic knowledge," the Society's mission is to inspire people to care about the planet. It reaches more than 400 million people worldwide each month through its official journal, *National Geographic*, and other magazines; National Geographic Channel; television documentaries; music; radio; films; books; DVDs; maps; exhibitions; live events; school publishing programs; interactive media; and merchandise. National Geographic has funded more than 10,000 scientific research, conservation, and exploration projects and supports an education program promoting geographic literacy.

For more information, please visit www.nationalgeographic.com, call 1-800-NGS LINE (647-5463), or write to the following address:

National Geographic Society, 1145 17th Street N.W., Washington, D.C. 20036-4688 U.S.A.

Visit us online at www.nationalgeographic.com/books

For librarians and teachers: www.ngchildrensbooks.org

More for kids from National Geographic: kids.nationalgeographic.com

For information about special discounts for bulk purchases, please contact National Geographic Books Special Sales: ngspecsales@ngs.org

For rights or permissions inquiries, please contact National Geographic Books Subsidiary Rights: ngbookrights@ngs.org

ISBN: 978-1-4263-1480-3

Printed in Hong Kong

14/THK/1